Mysteries of the Sun

Louella Bath

INFOMAX COMMON CORE READERS

Rosen Classroom™

New York

Published in 2014 by The Rosen Publishing Group, Inc.
29 East 21st Street, New York, NY 10010

Book Design: Mickey Harmon

Photo Credits: Cover, p. 11 (sun) Markus Gann/Shutterstock.com; pp. 3, 4, 6, 8, 10, 12, 14, 16, 18, 20, 23–24 (background) CS Stock/Shutterstock.com; p. 5 argus/Shutterstock.com; p. 7 (sun) Tamara Kulikova/Shutterstock.com; p. 7 (stars) Mihai-Bogdan Lazar/Shutterstock.com; p. 9 Milagli/Shutterstock.com; p. 11 (Earth) Cardens Design/Shutterstock.com; p. 13 Mike McDonald/Shutterstock.com; p. 15 djgis/Shutterstock.com; p. 17 Anna-Julia/Shutterstock.com; p. 19 Max Topchii/Shutterstock.com; p. 21 oorka/Shutterstock.com; p. 22 (background) Galyna Andrushko/Shutterstock.com.

ISBN: 978-1-4777-2593-1
6-pack ISBN: 978-1-4777-2595-5

Manufactured in the United States of America

CPSIA Compliance Information: Batch #CS13RC: For further information contact Rosen Publishing, New York, New York at 1-800-237-9932.

Contents

The Sun in the Sky

The sun is the biggest and brightest object in our **solar system**. We see it rise each day and set each night. Have you ever wondered why the sun is so important? It keeps us warm, gives us light, and helps plants live and grow. If the sun didn't exist, nothing on Earth would be able to survive—including us!

There are many cool facts to learn about the sun. For such an important object, it can sometimes seem mysterious. Uncovering these mysteries is a great way to understand our world.

Scientists believe the sun was formed about 4.6 billion years ago. One billion equals 1,000 millions!

Big and Bright

The sun is at the center of our solar system. Long ago, people believed Earth was the center, but now scientists know it's actually the sun. The sun's place at the center of the solar system affects everything around it.

The sun is a big, fiery star. It shines brighter than any other star in the sky. The sun seems bright to us because it's only about 93 million miles (150 million km) from Earth. You may not believe that's close, but it's much closer than any other star.

Not all stars look as bright as our sun. It's like when you see a light close-up compared to one that's far away. The closer one looks brighter.

People are naturally curious about what makes up the sun, since it's such a big part of our lives. The sun is made of gases–mostly hydrogen (HY-druh-juhn) and helium (HEE-lee-uhm). Most stars are made of these gases, too.

The sun has **layers**, just like Earth. Unlike Earth, there's no solid surface since it's made entirely of gases. Over many billions of years, gases came together to form different layers. The different layers of gas make the sun the biggest object in our solar system.

Can you name the different parts of the sun?

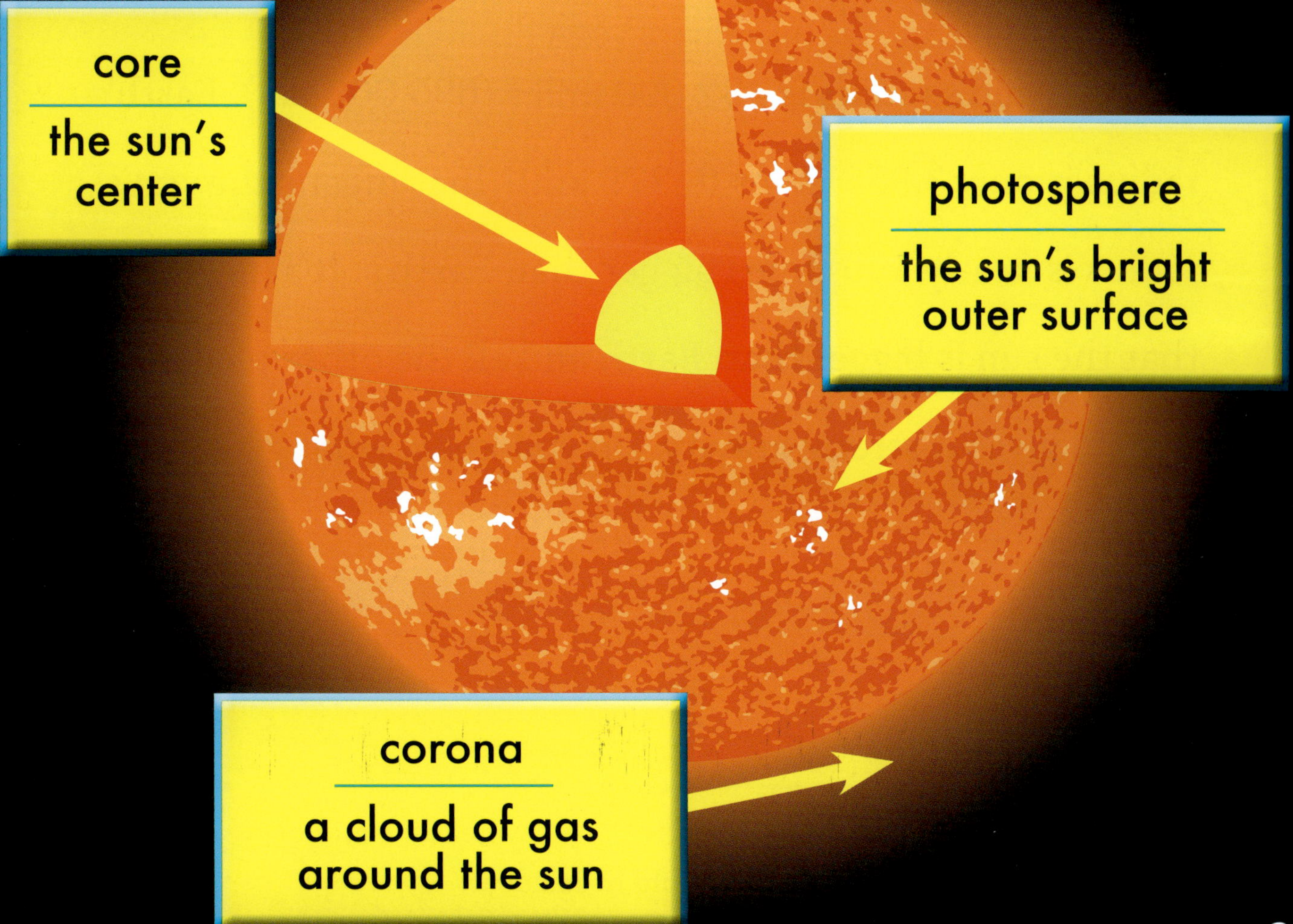
core
the sun's center
photosphere
the sun's bright outer surface
corona
a cloud of gas around the sun

Have you ever wondered how big the sun is? It's much bigger than Earth. You can tell by measuring its radius. The radius is the distance from the center of a circle or ball to a point on its outer surface.

The sun's radius is 432,000 miles (696,000 km). Earth's radius is only 3,955 miles (6,378 km)! That means the sun's radius is nearly 109 times bigger than Earth's. It's important that the sun is bigger than Earth and all the other planets. Its size gives it strong gravity. Do you know what gravity is?

The sun is so big that scientists say nearly 1 million Earths could fit inside it!

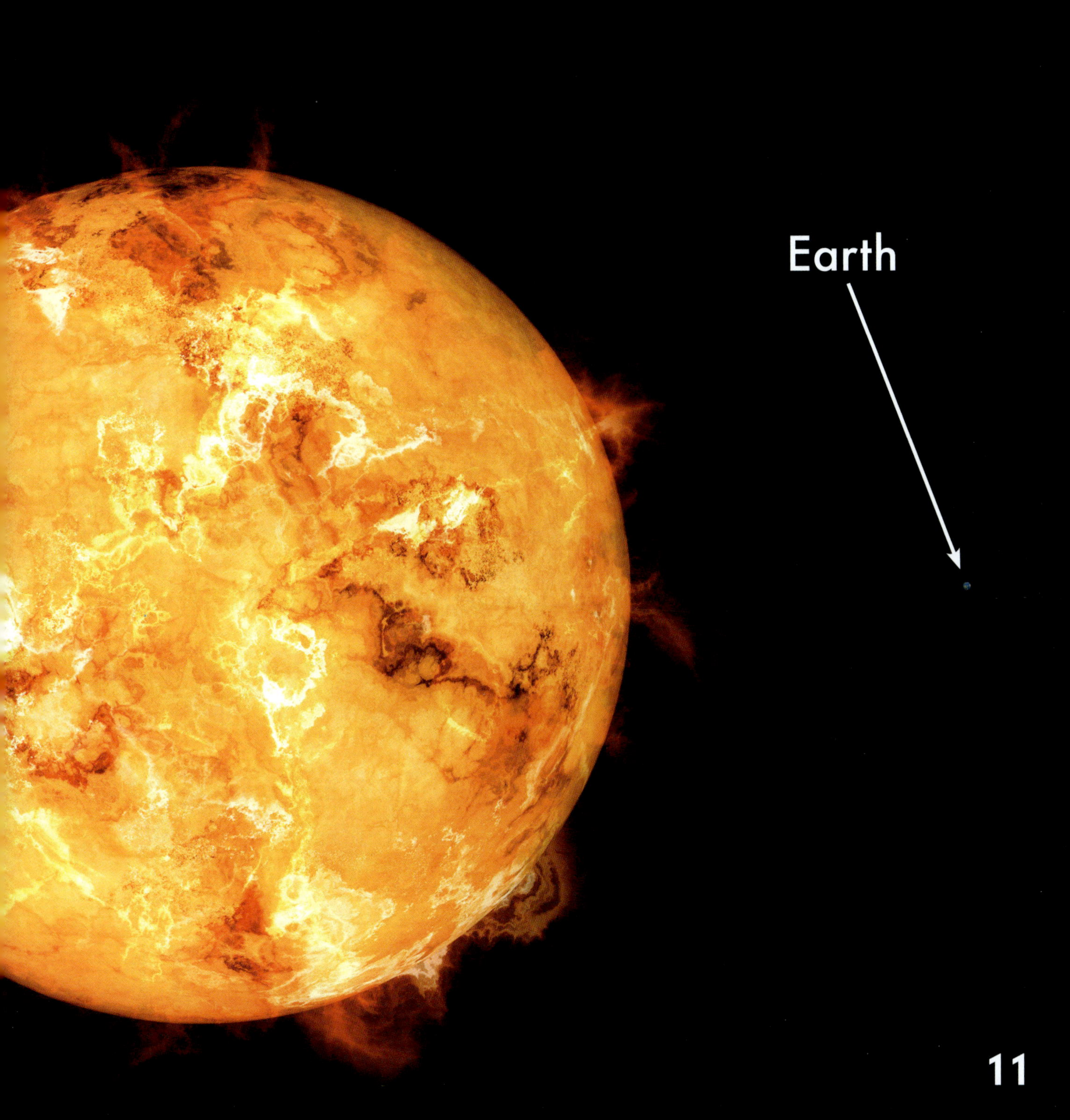
Earth

Gravity at Work

Gravity is the force that keeps Earth in place around the sun. The sun's force of gravity is much stronger than Earth's. Can you guess why? It's because the sun is so big. The more mass an object has, the greater its gravity.

The sun's gravity keeps everything in the solar system in place. If the sun's gravity didn't act upon Earth, Earth would spin off into space. Earth must stay in place to get heat and light from the sun.

You can imagine the sun as a big anchor that holds everything in the solar system in place.

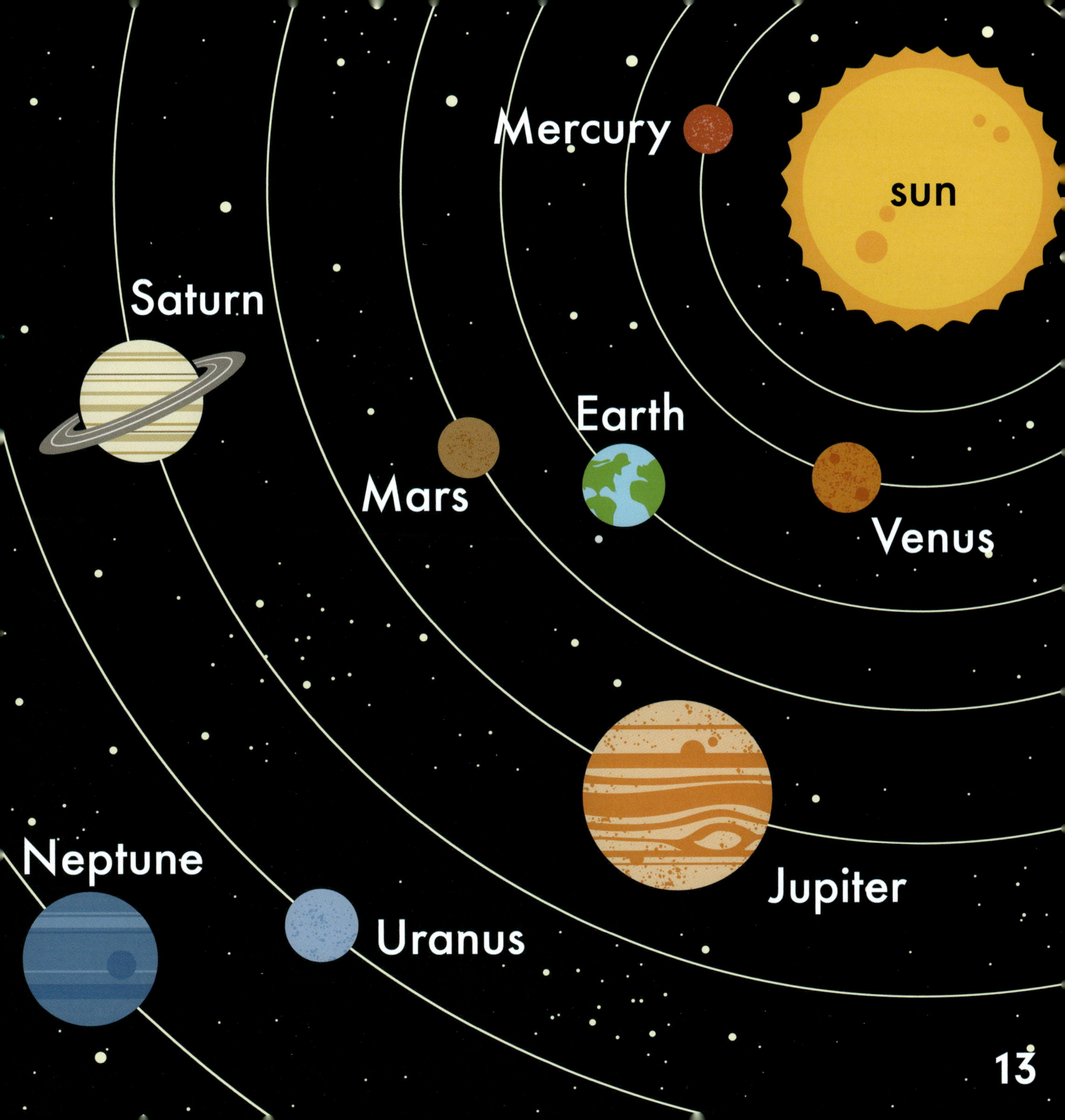
Mercury
sun
Saturn
Earth
Mars
Venus
Neptune
Jupiter
Uranus

Earth's position around the sun affects how much heat and light we get. It takes Earth one year to move completely around the sun. In that time, some parts of Earth are hot and others are cold. This depends on whether that part of Earth is learning toward or away from the sun.

Leaning toward the sun causes the sun's rays to hit Earth at an angle that makes it hot. Summer is hot because our part of Earth leans toward the sun. Winter is cold because our part of Earth leans away from it.

Have you ever heard what causes the sun to be so hot? Read on to find out!

So Hot!

Earth's **temperature** may change throughout the year, but the sun is always hot. The sun's surface temperature is around 10,300 degrees Fahrenheit (5,700 degrees Celsius). It's so hot that no one has ever been able to travel there. We would burn up!

Do you know what makes the sun hot? Hydrogen gas becomes helium gas in the sun's core. This change creates **energy** in the form of heat. There's so much heat energy that we can feel it even though we're millions of miles away.

Without the sun's heat, our planet would be as cold as ice and nothing would be able to survive.

All About Sunlight

The change of gases in the sun's core gives us another kind of energy–light energy. Light energy comes to Earth in the form of waves. The waves bounce off objects and then hit our eyes, allowing us to see. If the sun didn't give off light, we wouldn't be able to see anything.

Sunlight also helps plants make food. This is called photosynthesis (foh-toh-SIHN-thuh-suhs). Without sunlight, plants would die.

Never look directly at the sun.
It can really hurt your eyes.

Everyone knows it's light during the day and dark at night. But suppose something happens that causes it to be dark during the day. It's one of the sun's most interesting mysteries. It's called a solar eclipse (ih-KLIHPS).

A solar eclipse happens when the moon passes between Earth and the sun and blocks the sun from our view. This makes Earth dark for a few seconds. People used to be afraid of solar eclipses. They didn't understand what they were. Today, we look forward to seeing them!

Solar eclipses used to scare people. They thought it meant the sun was going away forever!

Still a Mystery

The sun is a big, burning star that affects all life on Earth, as well as almost everything else in our solar system. Because it affects us all, it's important to understand as much as we can about it.

We know more now than we ever have about how the sun works. There's still a lot to learn, though. Scientists are working very hard to learn new things about the sun, the most important object in our solar system!

Glossary

energy (EH-nuhr-jee) The power to do work.

layer (LAY-uhr) One thickness of something laying over another.

solar system (SOH-luhr SIHS-tuhm) The sun, planets, moons, and other space objects.

temperature (TEHM-puhr-chur) How hot or cold something is.

Index